Approaching Easter

Meditations for Lent

Joyce Huggett

D0801605

A LION BOOK

Tring · Batavia · Sydney

Published by
Lion Publishing plc
Icknield Way, Tring, Herts, England
ISBN 0 7459 1120 X (paperback)
ISBN 0 7459 1241 9 (casebound)
Lion Publishing Corporation
1705 Hubbard Avenue, Batavia, Illinois 60510, USA
ISBN 0 7459 1120 X
Albatross Books Pty Ltd
PO Box 320, Sutherland, NSW 2232, Australia
ISBN 0 86760 831 5

First edition 1987
Reprinted 1988

Acknowledgments

Bible quotations from *Good News Bible*, copyright 1966, 1971 and
1976 American Bible Society, published by the Bible Societies/
Collins; *Holy Bible, New International Version*, copyright 1978
New York International Bible Society; *The Jerusalem Bible*,
copyright 1966, 1967 and 1968 Darton, Longman, Todd and
Doubleday & Company Inc.; *The Living Bible*, copyright 1971
Tyndale House Publishers; *The New Testament in Modern English*,
copyright 1960 J.B. Phillips.

Other quotations as follows: William Barclay, *The Gospel of Luke*,
St Andrew Press, day 6; William Barclay, *The Gospel of Matthew*,
St Andrew Press, days 9, 37; Anthony Bloom, *Living Prayer*, Libra
Books, day 17; Corrie ten Boom *He Cares, He Comforts*, Lakeland
Paperbacks, day 25; Corrie ten Boom, *The Hiding Place*, Hodder &
Stoughton Ltd, day 23; Guy Brinkworth, *Thirsting for God*, Mullan
Press, day 15; Carlo Carretto, *Summoned by Love*, Darton,
Longman & Todd, day 14; Jim Cotter, *Prayer at Night*, Little Grove,
day 29; Alfred Edersheim, *The Life and Times of Jesus the Messiah*,
Longman, Green & Co. day 5; General Synod of the Church of
England, extracts from *The Alternative Service Book 1980*, day 46;
Michael Green, *I Believe in Satan's Downfall*, Hodder & Stoughton
Ltd. day 11; Stuart K. Hine, *How Great Thou Art*, Thankyou Music,
day 12; International Committee on English in the Liturgy, Inc.,
extracts from *The Roman Missal*, day 46; Julian of Norwich,
quoted in *Enfolded in Love*, Darton, Longman & Todd, day 16;
Michel Quoist, *Prayers of Life*, Gill & Macmillan Ltd, days 6, 11; Dan
Schutte, *Behold the Wood - A Dwelling Place*, North American
Liturgy Resources, day 40; Gilbert Shaw, *A Pilgrim's Book of
Prayers*, SLG Press, day 37; John Stott, *Men Made New*, IVP, day 30;
Desmond Sullivan, *The Way of the Cross*, Mayhew-McCrimmon Ltd,
day 38; William Temple, quoted in *Basic Christianity*, IVP, day 19;
Mother Teresa, quoted in *Something Beautiful for God*, Collins/
Fountain Books, days 22, 23; Jim Wallis, *The Call to Conversion*,
Lion Publishing, day 2.

Photographs by Robert Combs, day 16; Tony Deane, day 22;
Sonia Halliday Photographs: FHC Birch, day 40, Sonia Halliday,
days 5, 6, 24, 36, Laura Lushington, day 27, Jane Taylor, day 33;
Lion Publishing: David Alexander, day 9; Picturebank, day 3;
Jean-Luc Ray, day 38; Mick Rock: Cephas Picture Library, days 17,
31; Peter Stiles, day 20; David Townsend, day 19; ZEFA, days 1, 12,
13, 30

Printed and bound in Italy

Introduction

When I was a child, the playground at school would ring with two questions on Ash Wednesday: 'How many pancakes did *you* eat last night?' and 'What're *you* giving up for Lent?' From an early age, my answer to the second question was always the same: 'Sweets'. I never understood *why* I should go without sweets for six weeks of the year. But I did it willingly. It seemed expected of me by my parents and earned me the approval of my Sunday school teachers, so to my child-like way of thinking, it seemed a good thing to do.

I was well into my thirties before I learned why Christians down the ages practised self-denial during Lent; why, therefore, even as children, we had been encouraged to make small sacrifices in the weeks leading up to Easter. When the discipline was placed into its historical context for me, I was not only fascinated, I was thrilled: I could see that the potential for spiritual growth and renewal for those who submitted themselves to such discipline was immense.

It was a nun who explained to me that, originally, Lent was kept as a pre-Easter retreat: a prolonged period of time when Christians would 'tone up' spiritually. Their spiritual aerobics were not unlike the intensive training an athlete undergoes before an important race or the strict diet a person goes on in order to lose weight for medical or cosmetic purposes.

The reason why Christians took Lent so seriously from the days of the Early Church onwards is that Easter Day was the highlight of their year. On this day, like us, they celebrated the amazing fact that Jesus' body was not left in the grave to decay. He rose from the dead. But on this day they also welcomed converts to Christianity into the full fellowship of the church and welcomed back people who had once believed in God but whose faith in him had grown dim and whose love for him had grown cold. Throughout Lent, these people would prepare for Easter by becoming familiar with the basic teaching essential to an understanding of Christianity. They would be encouraged to repent of past failures and be shown how to live life God's way. Committed Christians did not escape the rigours of the Lenten season. They, too, took Lent seriously and used it as a time to examine their life-style, to turn their backs on the sin that so easily creeps into our lives and to re-dedicate their lives to God.

When I made this discovery, I determined to try this age-old recipe for spiritual fitness for myself. I would sacrifice, not sweets, but my most precious commodity, time: quality time for God. I would devote this time to extra prayer, extra Bible meditation, extra reflection and serious repentance. And I would see for myself whether this made a difference to the way I worshipped when Easter Day arrived.

I shall never forget the way God honoured that first true taste of Lenten discipline. He met me. He put his finger on inconsistencies in my life. He touched my perspective so that familiar Bible stories (Jesus' temptation in the wilderness, the Transfiguration, Gethsemane, the cross of Calvary) made a fresh impact on my mind, on my imagination and on my view of God. He touched my emotions so that I could respond to his love with fresh warmth and awe and gratitude.

Ever since that memorable spiritual highlight of my life, I have struggled to be especially still before God as Lent unfolds, not to recapture that original experience (God never does the same thing twice), but to give God space to go on changing me. But frequently I am frustrated because I find myself caught constantly in the web of my own busyness. For this reason, I have longed for a book which would encourage me to focus on God for a few minutes each day in Lent; which would also prepare my mind to be more receptive to what God is trying to say to me and do in me; which would challenge me to see Jesus afresh as Easter approaches. Such a book would need to make a visual impact on me because, so often, I find, God meets me through the visual: a sunset, a lighted candle, a beautiful view, a picture through which he can speak. Such a book would also need to place the spotlight on Jesus and the suffering he endured in the days leading up to Good Friday and on that memorable day itself because I find that familiarity with the facts of Christ's crucifixion can make me careless rather than attentive, casual rather than grateful. I need to be reminded from time to time just how much it cost him to die for me. And such a book would need to have some pages which I could read slowly; passages which are not designed to be read only once but rather invite the reader to savour the words and the images so that the hidden truths touch the emotions as well as the mind and the will.

As yet I have not found such a book. Instead, over the years and to meet my own particular needs, I have made a collection of readings, reflections and prayers. These have steered me through the bitter-sweet hours of Ash Wednesday, right through to the solemn days of Holy Week and into Easter Day itself.

In the pages that follow, I share a small selection of these reflections with readers who long similarly to anticipate Easter by preparing themselves in Lent; who are hungry for God also and want him to transform them in some way. My prayer is that the readings and the prayers, the meditations and the illustrations may inspire such people to focus fully on Jesus in the forty-day retreat of Lent so that we may all arrive at Easter Day prepared in spirit to encounter the living Christ afresh. If this should happen, then Lent will become for us what the church intended it to be: a 'holy spring': a time of prolific change and growth. And Easter Day will find us ready to rejoice with believers down the ages:
'I know that my Redeemer lives. I know that one day I shall see him for myself. I know that one day I shall be like him.'

Joyce Huggett

A time for
spiritual spring-cleaning

I love the first shafts of sunshine which burst through the windows in spring. Although they show up the layers of dust which have accumulated through the winter and challenge me to start spring-cleaning, they also herald the blossoming of new life: the wonder of spring.

The original meaning of Lent was 'holy spring'. Traditionally, at this time of year, Christians prepared themselves for Easter by asking God to show them their failures and by repenting of their wrong-doings. People new to Christianity were made ready for their baptism which would also take place at Easter. So Lent is a time of preparation: a spiritual spring-cleaning; a challenge to combat evil in

our lives. And Lent is a time to turn back to God. The prophet Joel puts the invitation this way:

> 'Come back to the Lord your God. He is kind and full of mercy; he is patient and keeps his promise; he is always ready to forgive and not punish.'
>
> Joel 2:13

> *Lord God, forgive me that so often I ignore the grime which soils my life: the grubby little sins collecting in the nooks and crannies of my heart, the cobwebs of guilt hanging from the walls of my life. Shine your Spirit's light into the dark, hidden crevices within me. Expose the murky fantasies, desires, ambitions and hopes which lurk there. Help me to deal ruthlessly with anything there which grieves you. Strengthen my resolve to go through with this internal spring-cleaning. And let me taste afresh your understanding, kind and patient love. Thank you that as I draw near to you, you are coming close to me.*

A time
for new beginnings

Lent is a time for new beginnings. New beginnings start with
repentance. Repentance is not negative. True repentance is an active,
positive attitude which effects real and deep changes. Repentance
involves recognizing the wrong, and, where possible, putting it right.
And when we repent we are determining in our minds that we will live
differently.

> John the Baptist said: 'Repent, for the kingdom of heaven
> is near.'
> Matthew 3:2

Repentance means to face up honestly to the past and to turn from
it . . .

'Our word *repentance* conjures up feelings of being sorry or guilty for
something. The biblical meaning is far deeper and richer. In the New
Testament usage, repentance . . . turns us from sin, selfishness,
darkness, idols, habits, bondages and demons both private and
public.

   'We turn from all that binds and oppresses us and others, from all
the violence and evil in which we are so complicit, from all the false
worship that has controlled us. Ultimately, repentance is turning from
the powers of death. These ominous forces no longer hold us in their
grip; they no longer have the last word.'
Jim Wallis

Repentance and receiving God's forgiveness go hand in hand.

> The apostle John writes: 'If we confess our sins to God, he
> will keep his promise . . . He will forgive us our sins and
> purify us from all our wrongdoing.'
> 1 John 1:9

When we have confessed, therefore, we must move on to receive and
embrace God's forgiveness and love. To fail to do so implies that we
give greater importance to our sinful self than to God's goodness. We
must learn to accept that God's goodness is greater than our badness;
that there is joy in God's heart in extending to us the forgiving love
which sets us free from past sin. So we must refuse to nurse a sense of
guilt and accept the healing God offers.

Father, thank you. Although I come to you sin-
stained and weary, hopelessly handicapped by my
own failures, I know you do not want me to nurse a
sense of guilt or inferiority but rather to shed my
burden so that I can be released and cleansed from
it. Here and now, I lay that burden at the foot of
your cross. There I leave it as I go to make amends
for the hurt I have caused.......................
and....................... May I love them with
your pure and reconciling love.

> Lord,
> You come to me
> You touch me
> You wipe away my tears
> You smile at me
> Embrace me
> You iron out my fears
> Thank you.

A time to come back

Lent is a glorious forty-day retreat. A retreat is a time to stand back; to ask: 'What have I been doing with my life? What has God been teaching me? Where have I succeeded in living life God's way? Where have I failed? What do I need to confess to God or to change?' A Lenten retreat is a time to recognize our wanderings and to determine to heed God's call to come back:

> 'But now, now – it is the Lord who speaks – come back to me with all your heart . . . turn to the Lord your God again, for he is all tenderness and compassion, slow to anger, rich in graciousness.'
>
> Joel 2:12,13

Like the young man in the story of the prodigal son, Lord Jesus, I make a calculated choice to come back to the Father:

> 'I will get up and go to my father and say, "Father, I have sinned against God and against you. I am no longer fit to be called your son: treat me as one of your hired workers . . .'

Like the young man in this story, I marvel at your response:

> 'He was still a long way from home when his father saw him; his heart was filled with pity, and he ran, threw his arms around his son, and kissed him . . . "Hurry!" he said. "Bring the best robe and put it on him. Put a ring on his finger and shoes on his feet . . . Let us celebrate with a feast!"'
>
> Luke 15

You are tender, compassionate, gracious and so slow to grow angry, O Lord. Thank you.

You are our peace, O Lord. From the thousand wearinesses of our daily life, from the disappointments, from the nervous and senseless haste, we turn to you and are at peace. The clamour dies, we are alive in the sunshine of your presence. Even so come, Lord Jesus, to this soul of mine.

A time to hope

Unending love is what God is. Lent is a time to experience that love all over again. For this reason, God 'woos' us and assures us that though we have failed him, he will not forsake us:

> 'How can I give you up? . . . How can I abandon you? . . .
> My heart will not let me do it! My love for you is too strong.'
> Hosea 11:8

Now is the time to make a personal response to God's invitation:

> 'Return to the Lord your God and let this prayer be your
> offering to him: "Forgive all our sins and accept our prayer,
> and we will praise you as we have promised."'
> Hosea 14:2

Because God's love is perfect, when we return to him, we enjoy security. He has promised that he will never abandon us nor banish us from his presence.

> 'Does a woman forget her baby at the breast,
> or fail to cherish the son of her womb?
> Yet even if these forget,
> I will never forget you.
> See, I have branded you on the palms of my hands.'
> Isaiah 49:15,16

With hope and confidence springing up afresh in our hearts we can
pray:

*Father in heaven, your love compels me, draws me
close. Hear the prayer of my heart. Let my cry of
repentance be received:*

Be merciful to me, O God,
    because of your constant love.
Because of your great mercy
    wipe away my sins!
Wash away all my evil
    and make me clean from my sin!
Remove my sin, and I will be clean;
    wash me, and I will be whiter than snow.
Let me hear the sounds of joy and gladness;
    and though you have crushed and broken me,
I will be happy once again.
Create a pure heart in me, O God,
    and put a new and loyal spirit in me . . .
Give me again the joy that comes from your salvation
    and make me willing to obey you . . .
Help me to speak, Lord,
    and I will praise you.
You will not reject a humble and repentant heart.
                                    Thank you.

> Child
> Place the fabric of your life
> In the vat of my love
> Watch
>   as I withdraw the stains of sin
> Know
>   that my grace makes you pure within
> Rejoice
>   for in me you will never be rejected
>   but always accepted
>   and uniquely loved.

The baptism of Jesus

Lent is a time to re-focus; to turn away from the business which pre-occupies us for most of the year and concentrate on Jesus. We start with his baptism. As Matthew describes it:

'Then Jesus came from Galilee to the Jordan to John to be baptized by him.'
Matthew 3:1

For thirty years Jesus had lived the life of an obscure carpenter in Nazareth. But he knew that his mission in life extended beyond the little town tucked away in the hills. He knew that he had come to rescue men and women from the tyranny of their own sin. When a wave of repentance swept through Galilee through the teaching of John the Baptist, Jesus chose that moment to make his first public appearance. Like hundreds of others, he was baptised by John. But unlike the others, he was not baptised as a sign that he repented of his sin. Jesus was sinless. He had no need to repent. Nevertheless, he identified with sinful mankind by descending into the green waters of the River Jordan. As he emerged from this beautiful river, he was deep in prayer. The heavens opened. The Holy Spirit fluttered down on him in the form of a dove. And he heard the Father's voice commissioning him: 'You are my Son, the Beloved'; in other words, 'You are the Messiah'.

Jesus knew that he was receiving the fulness of the Spirit to equip him for the task God had given him to do: to save the world from the clutches of the Evil One. He walked away from the river determined to build God's Kingdom on earth. He recognized that he was the Kingdom's 'Heaven-designated, Heaven-qualified, and Heaven-proclaimed King'.

To be the Messiah would involve suffering and death: death on a cross. Jesus knew that. Instead of flinching in the face of such pain, he accepted it out of love for his Father and for mankind. He knew that the only way to rescue mankind was to die in their place on the tree of Calvary.

Lord Jesus, when pain rises over the horizon
And threatens to engulf me
I recoil in terror
So I stand awe-struck as I watch you choose
Not life, but death
Not glory, but grief
Not joy, but sorrow
Not a crown, but a cross
And I marvel
For mine were the sufferings you carried
You were pierced through for my faults
Crushed for my sins
On you was being laid
A punishment that brings me peace
Because of your wounds
I enjoy healing
Such knowledge is too vast for me to grasp
But as I take it in
I worship you in wonder, love and praise.

The testing of Jesus

It has been said that temptation is the test which comes to a person whom God wishes to use. The word 'temptation' really means 'testing'. Just as metal has to be tested far beyond any strain or stress that will ever be placed on it before it can be considered reliable, so we have to be tested before God can use us in any major way. Lent is a time to observe closely the testings of Jesus. In the words of the apostle Matthew:

'Then Jesus was led by the Spirit into the desert to be tempted by the devil.'
Matthew 4:1

Jesus moves from the banks of the River Jordan into the wilderness where he was completely alone except for the wild beasts. He is steered from the devout acclaim of John the Baptist to the utter forsakenness of the desert. The audible approval of the heavenly Father is replaced by the vicious assaults of the devil. This fiercest of contests – between good and evil – took place in a desolate arena:

'The hills were like dust heaps; the limestone blistered and peeling; the rocks were bare and jagged; the ground sounded hollow to the horses' hooves; it glowed with heat like a vast furnace and it ran out to the precipices, one thousand, two hundred feet high which swooped down to the Dead Sea. It was there in that awesome devastation that Jesus was tempted'.
William Barclay

The person who attempts to live for God will be tested too:

'When a Christian has chosen to live for God and for others, the devil is not pleased. At certain times the din of temptation . . . returns more strident than ever. God allows this trial . . . in order to test him and to bring him to greater trust.'
Michel Quoist

At such times, we dare not 'go it alone'. We need God's help to keep us from falling:

'Lord –
Who can discern his errors?
Forgive my hidden faults.
Keep your servant also from wilful sins;
may they not rule over me . . .

May the words of my mouth and the meditation of my heart
be pleasing in your sight,
O Lord, my Rock and my Redeemer.'
Psalm 19:12-14

The self-denial of Jesus

In today's world we are familiar with the hunger strike through which a person or organization seeks to gain political power. We are accustomed, too, to people starving themselves to death to attract attention to a cause they believe in. For Jesus it was different. Matthew records:

> Jesus 'fasted for forty days and forty nights, after which he was very hungry.'
> Matthew 4:2

Many men and women before Jesus had fasted: Moses, the law-giver; King David; Queen Esther, to name a few. Such fasting in Bible times had one purpose only. People of God denied themselves food for a spiritual purpose: so that they could focus fully on God and his will. This is what Jesus is doing in the wilderness: giving himself to prayer, listening intently to his Father's instructions, seeking to discover how God wanted him to rescue mankind from the clutches of the Evil One.

While Jesus was concentrating on God in this way, Satan sidled up to him and did his utmost to dissuade Jesus from doing God's work in God's way. While he fasts, Jesus engages in 'spiritual warfare'.

The Christian, too, is caught up in a cosmic struggle against evil. The apostle Paul gives a clear warning of this salutary fact:

> 'For we are not fighting against human beings but against the wicked spiritual forces in the heavenly world, the rulers, authorities, and cosmic powers of this dark age.'
> Ephesians 6:12

The spiritual retreat of Lent challenges us to benefit from fasting also. By giving up a meal once a week, or all food for one day each week or denying ourselves the luxury of a television programme we enjoy, we, too, can give ourselves to leisurely prayer and listening to God. God will use this time to highlight inconsistencies in our life, to challenge us to change and to show us more of himself.

Lord Jesus, your humility and dedication to your Father's will disarm me. That you, the Son of God, went hungry and subjected yourself to the vicious assaults of the Enemy jolts me out of my false complacency. Teach me more of what it cost you to rescue me from the grip of Satan. Equip me to engage in the ongoing struggle against evil. Teach me how to gain the victory over temptation and evil.

Subtle persuasions

The wilderness where Satan and Jesus were engaged in spiritual warfare was littered with little bits of limestone which look rather like pitta bread: round and flat and creamy-white in colour. Since Jesus had not eaten for nearly six weeks, he was very hungry. Satan used that very moment to sidle alongside the Son of God to try to trip him up. As Matthew puts it:

> 'The tempter came and said to him, "If you are the Son of God, tell these stones to turn into loaves."'
>
> Matthew 4:3

The temptation was subtle and three-fold. Satan wanted Jesus to doubt his God-given identity so he taunts: '*If* you are the Son of God . . .' Satan also tries to persuade Jesus to use his God-endowed power selfishly and to win people by bribing them with material things. Jesus was not beguiled by any of these seemingly-sensible satanic suggestions. Instead he makes use of this temptation to select the methods he will use to win men back to God and which methods he will reject. Here he rejects once and for all the pathway to popularity, bribery and personal pleasure. He knows he is God's Son and he is determined to do God's work in God's way: by obeying God's word even though it involved accepting the way of suffering and, ultimately, death on the cross.

Satan uses the same ploys to trip up Christians today. He tries to persuade them that God cannot possibly love them. He tries to persuade them to use their talents, possessions and personalities for pure pleasure and self-gratification instead of dedicating them to God. There is no Christian who will not be tempted to use selfishly the talents entrusted to him by God. So the challenge of Lent comes to every Christian. St Theresa summed it up well: 'How long will it be before we imitate this great God in any way?'

> *Lord Jesus, your example fills me with admiration.*
> *Thank you that you won this round against Satan,*
> *thus setting me an example: to stand up to the devil*
> *when he whispers in my ear. Thank you that*
> *because you triumphed over evil, with your help, I*
> *can do the same.*

O Jesus, I have promised
To serve thee to the end;
Be thou for ever near me,
My Master and my Friend;
I shall not fear the battle
If thou art by my side,
Nor wander from the pathway
If thou wilt be my guide.

O let me feel thee near me·
The world is ever near;
I see the sights that dazzle,
The tempting sounds I hear;
My foes are ever near me,
Around me and within;
But, Jesus, draw thou nearer,
And shield my soul from sin.

John Ernest Bode

Subtle temptations

The Spirit of God had driven Jesus into the wilderness; the spirit of Satan now carries him to Jerusalem. Matthew describes it in this way:

> 'The devil then took (Jesus) to the holy city and made him stand on the parapet of the Temple. "If you are the Son of God" he said "throw yourself down . . ." Jesus said to him . . . "You must not put the Lord your God to the test."'
> Matthew 4:5-7

Jesus was standing on the pinnacle of the Temple, probably perched at the corner of the Temple looking down to the valley below – a sheer drop of four hundred and fifty feet. The time was probably daybreak so blasts from the priests' silver trumpets would be heralding a new day and Jerusalem would be thronging with people.

> 'Jump', taunts Satan. 'Let everyone see your Father catch you in his arms. Hasn't he promised to send his angels to watch over you in times of danger?'

If Jesus had leapt, like superman, from this pinnacle, his fame would have spread throughout Jerusalem. He would have won the applause, adulation and admiration of everyone. But Jesus refused to become a sensationalist by drawing attention to himself through the miracles he performed. He silenced the Enemy with the reminder from Scripture:

> 'Do not put the Lord your God to the test'.
> Matthew 4:7

'He meant this: there is no good seeing how far you can go with God; there is no good putting yourself deliberately into a threatening situation, and doing it quite recklessly and needlessly, and then expecting God to rescue you from it. . . God's rescuing power is not something to be played with and experimented with, it is something to be quietly trusted in the life of every day.'
William Barclay

Lord Jesus, you know the full force of temptation, yet you conquered it in the fight against Satan. Breathe into my life the strength of your Holy Spirit that I, too, may expose evil constantly, confront Satan valiantly and come out of conflict victoriously. In every moment of testing, may I stand fast as you did. In the challenge to combat evil in my life, may I grow neither faint nor weary but rather persevere to the end; until I hear your 'Well done, good and faithful servant.'

Subtle suggestions

Satan does not give up easily. He has tried to persuade Jesus to bribe people into the Kingdom of God by simply meeting their material needs; he has tried to encourage Jesus to attract attention to himself through the spectacular, to stoop to using magic to bring people to God. Having failed in both these attempts, Satan pesters Jesus with a third suggestion. Luke describes it in this way:

> 'Then leading him to a height, the devil showed him in a
> moment of time all the kingdoms of the world and said to him,
> "I will give you all this power and the glory of these
> kingdoms, for it has been committed to me and I give it to
> anyone I choose. Worship me, then, and it shall all be yours."
> But Jesus answered him, "Scripture says: 'You must worship
> the Lord your God, and serve him alone.'"'
> Luke 4:5-8

Jesus hadn't eaten for six weeks. He was weak physically. He knew that he faced the gargantuan task of winning the world for his Father; of snatching it back from the clutches of the Evil One. And Satan chose this moment of vulnerability to take Jesus out into God's wonderful world. There on a mountain top they viewed the splendour of God's creation in all its glory. How could one man capture all this for God?

Into Jesus' mind, Satan whispers an idea: 'Worship me and I will give all of this to you. Your task will be easy'.

What the tempter is whispering here may be summed up in one word, 'Compromise'. By stooping to the moral standards which the world accepts as the norm, Jesus could have attracted a great following! 'Why don't you strike a bargain with me?' suggests Satan. 'Change the world by becoming like the people who live in it. Then they will follow you in great numbers'.

Jesus' response to this suggestion is ruthless: 'Go away, Satan.' Jesus knew that he could never defeat evil by compromising with evil. He was called to be a light shining in the darkness of the world not to become a part of that darkness. His task was to raise men's standards until they were brought into perfect alignment with God's. Nothing less than that would do. Once again the result of this temptation is that Jesus submits himself to the Father. He determines to do God's work in God's way.

My little child
Relax!
Remember that I have branded you on the palms of my hands.
Remember that, though Satan would sift you like wheat,
I have asked the Father to protect you from the Evil One
Now
    and always.

Lord Jesus, thank you for revealing to us that you
endured these fierce assaults at the hand of the Evil
One. Thank you that because of your own
experience you can identify with us when we are
similarly tested. And thank you that you have
shown us how to overcome Satan. Give us the
courage we need to confront Satan and to banish
him from our presence. And give us such a love for
your Word, the Bible, that we may be able to use its
truth to expose the lies Satan whispers in our ears.
Give us the victory over Satan which you enjoyed,
that our effectiveness for you might increase.

Tempted! Just like me!

During Jesus' forty day retreat in the desert Satan aimed, in the words of Michael Green, to 'separate Jesus from his Father by doubt, by disobedience, by distrust, by disloyalty, by compromise, by exhibitionism, by idolatry and by short-circuiting Calvary.'

Today, Satan's target is Christians. They stand on Satan's firing line. But the author of the letter to the Hebrews reminds us that because he too was tempted, Jesus is able to help us:

> 'Because he has himself been through temptation he is able
> to help others who are tempted.'
>
> Hebrews 2:18

Satan is always on the rampage. The more we try to please God, the more he will seek to sidetrack us. As Peter puts it:

> 'Your enemy the devil is prowling round like a roaring lion,
> looking for someone to eat.'
>
> 1 Peter 5:8

Satan selects a variety of ways to bring about our downfall.

For example, he tests us through our feelings. On the days when we cannot feel God's presence he tries to persuade us that God has abandoned us; that he is a God who is more absent than present. He would even tempt us to doubt God's trustworthiness. These lies are to be rejected.

The tempter is also capable of using our innermost thoughts and desires to bring about our downfall. He launches his attack against our mind, our will and our passions so that even though we know that a certain course of action is not permissible for the Christian, we do it; even though we know that a certain place is riddled with temptation, we go there. And Satan wins another round in the eternal conflict between good and evil in our lives.

There are times when Satan confuses us so much that we don't know whether we want to obey God or not. Michel Quoist expressed this confusion powerfully in a prayer he once wrote:

I'm at the end of my tether, Lord.
I am shattered,
I am broken.
Since this morning I have been struggling to escape temptation,
   which, now subtle, now persuasive, now tender, now sensuous,
   dances before me like a glamour girl at a fair.
I don't know what to do.
I don't know where to go.
It spies on me, follows me, engulfs me.
When I leave a room I find it seated and waiting for me in the next . . .

The season of Lent challenges us to re-discover ways of combatting
the Enemy and triumphing over him as Jesus did. Jesus defeated
Satan by confounding his lies with the truth found in the Bible.
Martin Luther used to advise: 'The best way to drive out the devil if he
will not yield to texts of Scripture, is to jeer and flout him for he
cannot bear scorn.'

> *It seems almost a law of life, dear Lord, that after
> every great moment I experience I swing from the
> stars to the mud. And it is while I am struggling in
> the mud of my own defeat that Satan comes to me
> as the accuser using my weariness and
> discouragement, my moods and my depressions to
> cause me to doubt you. Teach me to resist the devil,
> Lord, just as you did. Cause me to be vigilant,
> conscious that he is ever ready to trip me up. May I,
> like you, triumph over him by submitting to the
> Father's will.*

The transfiguration

The Bible readings traditionally used by Christians during Lent move swiftly from focusing on the humanity of Jesus to the contemplation of his 'otherness', his divinity:

> 'Jesus took Peter, John, and James with him and went up a
> hill to pray. While he was praying, his face changed its
> appearance, and his clothes became dazzling white . . . While
> he was still speaking, a cloud appeared and covered them
> with its shadow; and the disciples were afraid as the cloud
> came over them. A voice said from the cloud, "This is my Son,
> whom I have chosen – listen to him!"'
> Luke 9:28,29,34,35

Even today, the Mount of Transfiguration fills some people with awe as they meditate on this miraculous moment in the life of Jesus. There one can imagine the cloud descending, indicating how near God was. One can imagine the sound of the Father's voice proclaiming how much he loved and appreciated his Son. And one can contemplate the transfigured form of Jesus: his body enveloped with the light of God, his face radiating the glory of God and his clothing shining with a whiteness the human eye could scarcely tolerate.

Lent provides us with the challenge and opportunity to drink in these mysteries: the mystery of who God is, the mystery of his greatness, the mystery of his humility in taking on himself a human form. As we take time out to focus on the mysteries, our hearts are filled with awe and wonder and praise.

> *Lord Jesus, just as you took your friends with you to
> the top of the mountain and there revealed your
> glory, may I, too, draw close to you to receive the
> perception to see you in your holiness, worship you
> for who you are and learn to listen to you: through
> your Word, the Bible, through silence, through
> nature.*

O Lord my God! When I in awesome wonder
Consider all the works thy hands have made,
I see the stars, I hear the mighty thunder,
Thy power throughout the universe displayed.
Then sings my soul, my Saviour God, to thee:
How great thou art! How great thou art!

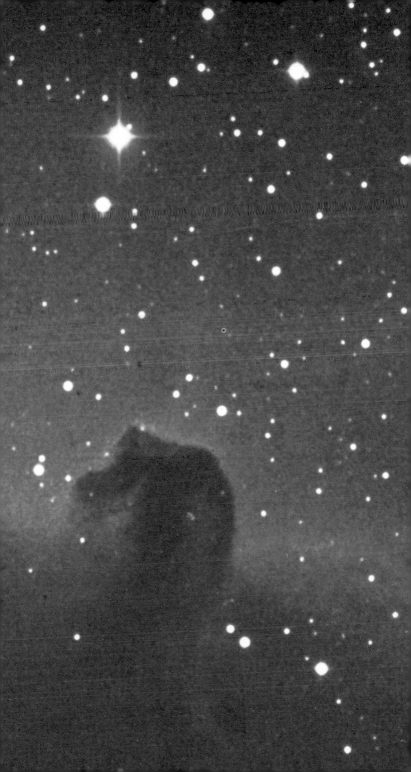

Lord, teach us to pray

Jesus' disciples could see for themselves that the quality of Jesus' prayer was different from any form of prayer they had encountered before. One day they begged him:

> 'Lord, teach us to pray.'
> Luke 11:1

Lent, the special season set apart for reflection and prayer, is a good time to reiterate that request and to act on Jesus' basic advice:

> 'When you pray, go to your private room and, when you have shut your door, pray to your Father who is in that secret place.'
> Matthew 6:6

People who are serious about learning to pray hold two things in tension: the fact that it is possible to pray at any time and in any place and the fact that there is great value in heeding Jesus' advice and ear-marking a certain place for regular prayer. That place might be a corner of the bedroom, a certain chair in the study, a quiet room in the house, a church or a particular walk or spot in the garden. We know that when we retreat to that place it is for one purpose only: the serious business of prayer.

Prayer, essentially, is developing a relationship with God. Friends find time and places to meet. If we are serious about forging a friendship with God, we will do what he says: prepare a meeting place where the friendship can grow and deepen. The more we meet God in the silence of this specific place of prayer, the more we shall learn to recognize his presence elsewhere: in nature, while walking or driving, ironing, gardening or talking to friends and neighbours.

Dear Lord, teach me to pray
For just as the deer pants for cool water
So my heart hungers for you
My soul is parched and dry
I thirst for the presence of the living God.
I will carve out a place for you.
Lord, hear my prayer.
In that place
In every place
Come to me and meet me.

To pray like Jesus

In answer to the disciples' request: 'Lord, teach us to pray', Jesus said:

'Say this when you pray: Father'
Luke 11:2

No one had ever prayed like Jesus before because no one in the whole world had ever been conscious, as he was, that God was his Father, that God's love for him was total. When Jesus prayed, he frequently referred to God as 'Abba' – Father, Daddy. Jesus implores his disciples to do the same: to turn childlike, trusting eyes to God and simply to whisper: 'Daddy'.

A good father cherishes his child, provides security, stability, guidance and unconditional love. A good father makes sacrifices for his child. A good father delights in every stage of his child's growth. God is a good father. As Carlo Carretto puts it:

'God is my father and looks after me.
God is my father and loves me . . .
With him I have the gift of life
With him I have the gift of truth.
With him I have the gift of love . . .
If God is my father, I can be calm and live in peace;
I am secure for life, for death, for time and for eternity . . .
If God is my father, I count for something and in him find my own true dignity . . .
God is God of the universe, even when the earth quakes and the rivers overflow, and he is my father, even if my hands get frost-bite and an accident makes me a cripple for life.'
Carlo Carretto

Because God is my Father, and because prayer is the place where, consciously, I call him Father, prayer is, supremely, the place where I know myself to be loved and held and met by God. In prayer I am conscious that God the Father comes to me, wipes away my tears, heals my hurts and enfolds me in his love.

Father
In this place of prayer
I feel your everlasting arms
Enfolding me
Caressing me
Cradling me
In the embrace of never-ending love.
For this tenderness
I praise you
That I am the focus of your love.
I thank you
That you have deigned to call me your child.
I adore you
And surrender myself to you
Though all too feeble
Is my response of love to Love.

Father,
I abandon myself into your hands;
do with me what you will.
Whatever you may do, I thank you:
I am ready for all, I accept all.
Let only your will be done in me,
and in all creatures.
I wish no more than this, O Lord.
Into your hands I commend my soul:
I offer it to you
with all the love of my heart,
for I love you, Lord, and so need to give myself,
to surrender myself into your hands,
without reserve,
and with boundless confidence,
for you are my Father.

Charles de Foucauld

A unique relationship

A vital ingredient of any developing friendship is time. If our relationship with God is to develop, grow and mature, it is essential that we give God quality time. During Lent, many Christians make sacrifices to increase the amount of time available for undivided attention to God. Jesus tells us what to do with this time:

'You should pray like this: "Our Father in heaven, may your name be held holy . . ."'
Matthew 6:9

God's name is much more than a brand or label. It involves his entire personality. This word holy means 'different', 'unique'.

So Jesus seems to be suggesting that in our thinking and relating, God's personality should be treated differently from all other personalities. God's personality should be given a position which is absolutely unique. In other words, God is to be reverenced.

If we apply this phrase from the Lord's Prayer to ourselves, it will mean that we live our lives in a constant awareness of God. The world will seem so God-filled that our hearts will be filled with awe as we are reminded of his greatness, his tenderness, his compassion and his love. Nature will give us these reminders; so will the face and trust of a child; and so might the joy of someone caught up in the worship of God.

Lent is the season to concentrate on increasing our ability to be conscious of God's presence by our side:

'As I work, a Loved Presence over my shoulder, as I drive, a Loved Passenger beside me; in my reading, cooking, studying; whilst teaching, nursing, accounting; in the maelstrom of the supermarket or waiting for the bus or train – ever the loving sense of a Presence – always the nostalgia for my Creator.'
Guy Brinkworth

Father
Holy
Revered
Mysterious is your Name
May all my contacts and relationships
My struggles and temptations
My thoughts, dreams and desires
Be coloured by the loving reverence I have for you.
May your personality be reflected
In my work
In the words of my lips
And in the thoughts which lodge in my mind
So that all I am
And all I do
May become ever more worthy of your holy presence
Living in me.

God be in my head and in my understanding
God be in my eyes and in my looking
God be in my mouth and in my speaking
God be in my tongue and in my tasting
God be in my lips and in my greeting . . .
God be in my ears and in my hearing
God be in my neck and in my humbling . . .
God be in my hands and in my working . . .
God be at my end and at my reviving.

Your will be done

When Jesus was coaching his disciples in the art and the ABC of praying, he said:

> 'You should pray like this: . . . your will be done.'
> Matthew 6:9,10

At the nub of true prayer lies obedience. In fact, one can scarcely think about prayer without thinking about obedience. Obedience means the relinquishment of *my will* – my longings, my desires, my choices – and the acceptance of God's will. Obedience involves my will being brought into complete alignment with the will of God.

Jesus could teach others this prayer of obedience because he was obedient to his Father in every detail of his life. Indeed, Jesus delighted to submit his will to the Father's will. Rather he knew that his Father's will was not something menacing. He knew that his Father's will had his best intentions at heart. Far from wanting to escape from it, he took it on board, even when it hurt him to do so. This kind of obedience demonstrates the faith he had in the fact that God's plans are always loving and right.

The father of a new-born baby once expressed to me his feelings for his wife and child:

'I've never loved anyone like this before. I can think of no one but them. I just want to be with them doing whatever I can for them. When they are distressed, I am distressed. When they are happy, I am happy. Nothing else matters to me at the moment – only them.'

The biblical notion of the will of God is like that. It means that God's longing and desire, love and joy are focused on his people. He delights in them. He safeguards them. He yearns over them. That is why the Christian can say with confidence, in the words of Julian of Norwich: 'I saw that he is to us everything that is good.'

> *'Lord, you know what I desire, but I desire it only if it is your will that I should have it. If it is not your will, good Lord, do not be displeased, for my will is to do your will.'*
> Julian of Norwich

Forgive us . . .

as we forgive

When the disciples asked Jesus to teach them how to pray, he gave them clear instructions:

> 'You should pray like this: . . . "Forgive us the wrongs we have done as we forgive the wrongs that others have done to us."'
>
> Matthew 6:12

Jesus adds a warning to these strict instructions:

> 'If you forgive others the wrongs they have done to you, your Father in heaven will also forgive you. But if you do not forgive others, then your Father will not forgive the wrongs you have done.'
>
> Matthew 6:14

Of course, we should be obeying these exhortations of Jesus all the year round, but many of us live life at such a pace that it is all too easy to fail to recognize where lack of forgiveness has taken up residence in our hearts. Now is an excellent opportunity to ask God to put his finger on any relationship which has turned sour or on any bitterness or resentment against people which has been poisoning our lives. When he places his spotlight on such emotions, we must tip out the rubble which has collected in our lives so that God can fill us anew with his life.

It is important that we understand what forgiveness is and what it is not.

Forgiveness is not a matter of warm emotions. It is a function of the will. It is asking the question not *can* I forgive but *will* I forgive, the Lord being my helper.

And forgiveness is not pretending that a particular person has not injured or upset us in some way. True forgiveness entails recalling the full extent of the hurt inflicted and admitting: 'Yes, that hurt', but then moving on from there, determining: 'Nevertheless I will forgive because God requires it of me.'

To forgive means to let go of resentments, bitterness, hatred, unnecessary anger; to let it drop out of our lives. To forgive means to let a person off the hook. To forgive means to cancel the debt we feel we are owed. It can be done, but only with God's help.

'Forgiveness is something extremely difficult to achieve . . . What we call forgiveness is often putting the other one on probation, nothing more; and lucky are the forgiven people if it is only probation and not remand. We wait impatiently for evidence of repentance, we want to be sure that the penitent is not the same any more, but this situation can last a lifetime and our attitude is exactly the contrary of everything which the gospel teaches, indeed commands us to do . . . We cannot go further if we are not forgiven, and we cannot be forgiven as long as we have not forgiven every one of those who have wronged us. This is quite sharp and real and precise . . .'
Anthony Bloom

My child
I see the pockets of poison which have collected inside you.
Here and now
I lance the abscess
Drain it of its pus,
And cleanse you through and through.
Receive my love afresh.
Let it wash right through you
And cleanse you
Carry it to those you secretly despised.
My love alone bears the healing grace of reconciliation.

> 'O Lord, my God, I cried to you for help, and you have
> healed me.'
>
> Psalm 30:2

Thank you.

*Lord, I want this Lent to be a true preparation for
Easter: a letting out of all that cannot co-exist with
your love in my life. As I re-read your challenge:
'Forgive! Forgive! Forgive!' I am aware that I have
been withholding forgiveness from . . . .
. . . . and . . . . and . . . . . .
. . . . because of . . . .
Because you require it of me, my dear Lord, I forgive
them now. I let them off the hook. Forgive me that I
have borne this grudge for so long. See in my heart
the poison of bitterness, resentment and hatred
which I have stored there, fingering it from time to
time thus gaining sick pleasure from past
grievances. Here and now, before you, the living
God, I repent of my negativeness and beg your
forgiveness.*

Praying now

Jesus' life and ministry of prayer did not stop when he ascended to heaven. The writer to the Hebrews assures us that Jesus' prayer-life is ever active and ever effective:

> 'He is able, now and always, to save those who come to God through him, because he lives for ever to plead with God for them.'
> Hebrews 7:25

> 'Christ . . . entered . . . heaven itself, so that he could appear in the actual presence of God on our behalf.'
> Hebrews 9:24

Jesus' prayer life on earth was unique. His prayer-life today is more amazing still. I like to have written up in my study: 'Jesus is praying for me now.' The thought that Jesus is stationed in heaven at the throne of the Father where he prays for us continuously is an awesome one. But this is Jesus' ongoing ministry. Because he is ever the man of prayer, when we pray, we can, as it were, come alongside him, stand with him in the Father's presence, break through the limitations of time and space and be assured that our prayers are both heard and honoured.

Lent disciplines us to carve out time for this priceless privilege of praying alongside the man of prayer, Jesus himself.

> *Lord, it fills me with wonder that you have given to me the privilege of drawing alongside you in the awesome work of prayer. The very thought is humbling. Forgive me that I take so little advantage of this privilege. May I drink in this truth for myself in such a way that, day by day, I come to you to intercede for the needs of the world, the needs of my friends, the needs of my neighbours. Continue to teach me to pray. May I go on learning from you until I have mastered the art of effective prayer; until I have learned to pray as you pray.*

You are Three and One,
    Lord God, all good.
    You are good, all good, supreme good,
    Lord God, living and true.
You are love,
    You are wisdom.
    You are humility,
    You are endurance.
    You are rest,
    You are peace.
    You are joy and gladness.
    You are justice and moderation.
    You are all our riches,
    And you suffice for us.
You are beauty.
    You are gentleness,
    You are our protector,
    You are our guardian and defender.
    You are courage.
    You are our haven and our hope.
You are our faith,
    Our great consolation.
    You are our eternal life,
    Great and wonderful Lord,
    God almighty,
    Merciful Saviour.
    St Francis of Assisi

The harvest of the Spirit

One cold, grey November day I was asked to meet a friend from the station in the town where I live. When I arrived, to my surprise, the normally-cheerless foyer of the station had been completely transformed. A woman wearing a brightly-coloured dress had set up a fruit and flower stall. On it she had piled rows of red apples alongside bunches of ripe, yellow bananas; orange tangerines alongside clusters of green grapes; scarlet tomatoes alongside amber pineapples. This fruit, together with the purples and pinks and whites and maroons of Christmas chrysanthemums, not only brought a splash of colour to brighten the drabness of the day and the building, it also filled the air with fragrance.

Paul suggests that the life of the Christian should be equally attractive, equally cheering and equally fragrant. He describes the cluster of qualities which should characterize our lives:

'Love
    joy
        tranquillity
            forbearance with others
                kindness
                    generosity
                        reliability
                            humility
                                self-control'

The reason why Jesus' personality and ministry were so magnetic was that in him each of these characteristics had been perfected. Towards God he was utterly loving. This love was demonstrated in his willingness to obey the Father in everything. His love for God and trust in him were so complete that his chief joy in life was his relationship with the Father and no matter what happened to him he remained unruffled, tranquil.

Towards other people Jesus was kind, generous, reliable and forgiving. And such was his self-control that he never 'lost his cool'.

What Paul is saying to Christians is: You be like that. He reveals the secret of success in this seemingly impossible task by showing that this spiritual perfection is the fruit of the Holy Spirit introduced into our lives. Without God's Spirit, these qualities will not mature in us. But if the root of the Spirit is present, the fruit must ripen. In the words of Jesus, in Matthew 7:7: 'Every good tree bears good fruit.'

'It is no good giving me a play like Hamlet or King Lear, and telling me to write a play like that. Shakespeare could do it; I can't. And it is no good showing me a life like the life of Jesus and telling me to live a life like that. Jesus could do it; I can't. But if the genius of Shakespeare could come and live in me, then I could write plays like that. And if the Spirit of Jesus could come and live in me, I could live like that.'
William Temple

The good news is that the Spirit of Jesus has come. His equipping and empowering are available for those who ask:

'God has poured out his love into our hearts by the Holy
Spirit, whom he has given us.'
Romans 5:5

Even so this spiritual fruit in us ripens slowly. Let's ask God to increase his effectiveness in us as this coming week we look in detail at the kind of life he wants us to live.

Lord –
You examine me and know me,
you know if I am standing or sitting,
you read my thoughts from far away,
whether I walk or lie down, you are watching,
you know every detail of my conduct . . .
Examine me and know my heart,
probe me and know my thoughts;
make sure I do not follow pernicious ways,
and guide me in the way that is everlasting.
Psalm 139:1-3;23,24

A useful thermometer

Self-examination is rather like taking your spiritual temperature. Paul's description of the harvest of the Spirit provides a useful thermometer for such purposes.

> 'The Spirit brings . . . love, joy, peace, patience, kindness, goodness, trustfulness, gentleness and self-control.'
> Galatians 5:22,23

If we examine these qualities one by one and compare our lives with these spontaneous manifestations of the Spirit's presence, we shall quickly discover the kind of prayer we need to pray in order that we might become more Christ-like in our behaviour and attitudes.

Today we focus on gentleness.

One year I sustained head and back injuries in a car crash in Yugoslavia. I discovered that to be hospitalized in a country where few people speak your language can be a traumatic experience. I also discovered the healing properties of gentleness. A Yugoslav doctor used to sit by my bedside in his off-duty time and try to communicate with me in broken English. The elderly women who were my fellow-patients were unable to communicate with me verbally, but each evening, before lights-out, they would come and gently kiss my forehead. Such gestures of kindness brought me deep consolation and a sense of well-being.

In the harsh, brash world in which we live, the implication is that gentleness will get you nowhere. But the Bible teaches that gentleness is one of the signs that God's Spirit is at work in us.

Those of a gentle spirit are those who are considerate, courteous and kind. The whole idea of gentleness is a kindness which expresses itself in active service to meet the perceived needs of others. What is more, the gentle person is so concerned with the feelings and well-being of others that he or she will never cause needless hurt and will never resort to rudeness, abruptness or abrasiveness. Even when the gentle person has to be firm, this firmness will be laced with compassion, tenderness, and the self-control without which these qualities would be impossible.

> *Heavenly Father, thank you for the gentleness I see*
> *in the people around me. Thank you especially for*
> *........................ and ....*
> *I covet this fruit of through-and-through kindness,*
> *Lord. Please cause this fruit to mature and mellow*
> *in me that I, too, may become increasingly gentle in*
> *my dealings with others; that my words and even*
> *my thoughts might manifest this lovely quality: the*
> *gentle spirit.*

Spiritual fruit:love

Just as a healthy vine will produce good grapes, so a Christian who is full of the Spirit's life will produce spiritual fruit.

Today we concentrate on Paul's claim:

'The fruit of the Spirit is love.'
Galatians 5:22

The love Paul mentions here is not the pop-song, Hollywood, romantic variety: love trivialized and commercialized. It is Jesus' love: the unselfish affection and unceasing activity which seeks only the well-being of the loved one; the love which is born from the desire to meet the person's deepest needs and to promote his or her growth. This love is inextinguishable. No matter what a person may have done to insult or injure or humiliate us, we will seek only his highest good. This dimension of love affects the mind and the will even more than the emotions:

'Love is patient, love is kind. It does not envy, it does not boast, it is not proud. It is not rude, it is not self-seeking, it is not easily angered, it keeps no record of wrongs . . . It always protects, always trusts, always hopes, always perseveres.
Love never fails.'
1 Corinthians 13:4,5,7,8

Our model for this kind of love-in-action is Jesus. Time after time his disciples let him down and failed to understand his mission. Nevertheless as Jesus prepares to leave them he expresses unending love for them. This love is extended to all mankind and was supremely demonstrated in Jesus' death at Calvary:

'God demonstrates his own love for us in this: While we were still sinners, Christ died for us.'
Romans 5:8

Lord Jesus
I marvel at your healing, self-giving love.
When I am hurt
Or neglected
Or when friends fail to respond to my love,
I withdraw,
Cold,
Silent,
Prickly,
Bruised.
But your love never gives up.
You see the one you love
And think, not of your own needs,
But of his need to be restored
And loved.
Teach me to give as you give;
To love as you love.
Produce in me a qualitative love –
    which is always in season.

*'Lord, grant that I may seek rather to comfort than
to be comforted; to understand than to be
understood; to love than to be loved; for it is by
forgetting self that one finds; it is by dying that one
awakens to eternal life.'*
From a prayer attributed to St Francis of Assisi

More spiritual fruit: joy and kindness

Mother Teresa of Calcutta, who has dedicated her life to rescuing the deprived and dying in one of India's worst slums, radiates joy even when she is confronted with poverty, stench and intolerable need. The apostle Paul says:

> 'What the Spirit brings is . . . joy.'
> Galatians 5:22

Joy is much more than a fleeting feeling. It is the ability to rejoice in spite of difficult places, difficult people or persistent pain. Joyful people have burrowed their roots into the soil of God's love:

'Joy is a net of love by which you can catch souls.'
'She gives most who gives with joy.'
'The best way to show our gratitude to God and the people is to accept everything with joy.'
'A joyful heart is the normal result of a heart burning with love.'
'Never let anything so fill you with sorrow as to make you forget the joy of Christ Risen.'
Mother Teresa

When the Holy Spirit is active in our lives, he also produces within us the fruit of kindness:

> 'What the Spirit brings is . . . kindness.'
> Galatians 5:22

'Let no one even come to you without coming away better and happier. Be the living expression of God's kindness to the poor. To children, to the poor, to all who suffer and are lonely, give always a happy smile. Give them not only your care, but also your heart.'
Mother Teresa

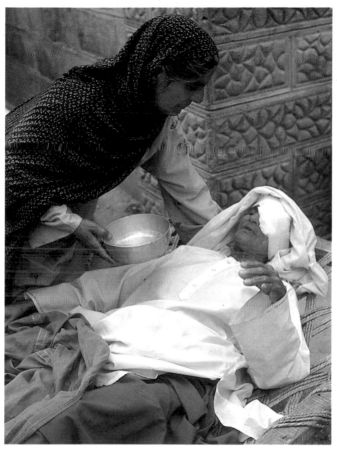

Lord Jesus, you know me well enough to know that it is not always joy which characterizes my life. Very often despondency, disappointment and dissatisfaction with my lot in life obliterate my joy, just as thunder-clouds blot out the glory of the sun's rays. You know, too, that there are occasions when I don't even want to be kind: indeed, I consider it my right to hate, to point the finger and to withhold love. Forgive me, Lord. How unlike you I am. How much work the Spirit has yet to do to change me into your likeness. Continue this transforming work in me, though, Lord. Chip away at the sculpture of my life until like Jesus I am consistently kind in a cruel world.

Peace

The need for peace in the world is more urgent now than ever before. Peace starts in the heart of the individual and then spreads from one person to another.

'Let us radiate the peace of God and so light his light and extinguish in the world and in the hearts of all men, all hatred, and love for power.'
Mother Teresa

Jesus said:

> 'Peace is what I leave with you; it is my own peace that I
> give you.'
> John 14:27

And Paul said:

> 'The Spirit produces . . . peace.'
> Galatians 5:22

The peace which is spoken of here is the ability to remain calm, tranquil and serene in every circumstance because we entrust our life and loved ones to the wisdom, sovereignty and protective care of God. It is the kind of quality of life which the Dutch Christian Betsie ten Boom demonstrated in the concentration camp at Ravensbruck. Although her father had been tortured and murdered and although she and her sister endured intolerable conditions in the camp, peace so controlled her that she was able to bring comfort and joy to the women who were fellow-prisoners with her. Peace so pervaded her spirit that she transformed the foul cell which she shared with crowds of other women.

'The straw pallets were rolled instead of piled in a heap, standing like pillars along the walls, each with a lady's hat atop it. A headscarf had somehow been hung along the wall. The contents of several food packages were arranged on a small shelf . . . Even the coats hanging on their hooks were part of the welcome of that room, each sleeve draped over the shoulder of the coat next to it like a row of dancing children.'
Corrie ten Boom

Peaceful people do not need to *speak* about Christ, they radiate his love and his likeness:

'For me, 'twas not the truth you taught
To you so clear, to me so dim
But when you came to me you brought
A sense of him
And from your eyes he beckons me
And from your heart his love is shed
Till I lose sight of you, and see
The Christ instead.

> *Heavenly Father, fill me afresh with your Holy Spirit*
> *that people may watch the way I live and see, not*
> *me, but you shining through me.*

Peace, perfect peace, in this dark world of sin?
The blood of Jesus whispers peace within.

Peace, perfect peace, by thronging duties pressed?
To do the will of Jesus, this is rest.

Peace, perfect peace, with loved ones far away?
In Jesus' keeping we are safe, and they.

Peace, perfect peace, our future all unknown?
Jesus we know, and he is on the throne.

Peace, perfect peace, death shadowing us and ours?
Jesus has vanquished death and all its powers.

It is enough: earth's struggles soon shall cease,
And Jesus call us to heaven's perfect peace.
Edward Henry Bickersteth

Show us, good Lord,
    the peace we should seek,
    the peace we must give,
    the peace we can keep,
    the peace we must forgo,
and the peace you have given in Jesus our Lord.

Patience

There was once a Scottish school teacher who endeared himself to his pupils with his patience. Whenever a child submitted a piece of work to him which was ink-stained, this teacher would draw round the blob of ink and create from it an angel before handing the corrected piece of work back to the boy or girl concerned. This generous gesture encouraged many careless pupils to want to change.

Such acceptance of people's weaknesses does not come naturally to most of us. But it is a quality of life which Paul, in his letter to the Galatians, encourages us to acquire. 'The fruit of the Spirit is patience.' The patience mentioned here is patient endurance, and refers chiefly to our relationships with people. This patience is the generosity a person displays when he or she could take revenge against someone who has injured or insulted or hurt them but who chooses not to do so. We see this kind of patience modelled to us most perfectly by Jesus:

'(Jesus) was oppressed and afflicted,
yet he did not open his mouth;
he was led like a lamb to the slaughter,
and as a sheep before her shearers is silent,
so he did not open his mouth.'
Isaiah 53:7

'When (Jesus) was accused by the chief priests and the elders, he gave no answer. Then Pilate asked him, "Don't you hear how many things they are accusing you of?" But Jesus made no reply, not even to a single charge – to the great amazement of the governor.'
Matthew 27:13,14

Lord Jesus, thank you for the example which you have set me. I want to learn to be as patient with others as you are with me. Pour into my heart the spirit of tolerance, acceptance and unquenchable love for others. When friends let me down, or people fail to live up to my expectations, keep me from withdrawing my affection, as I so easily do. Help me, instead, to go on loving and praying and trying to understand.

O Love that wilt not let me go,
I rest my weary soul in Thee:
I give Thee back the life I owe,
That in Thine ocean depths its flow
May richer, fuller be.

George Matheson

Be filled with the Spirit

Corrie ten Boom, who became a world-famous evangelist after her release from the Ravensbruck Concentration Camp, tells of an occasion when God transformed her attitude and behaviour. She was speaking at a meeting in Germany. One women in the meeting seemed unable to look into Corrie's eyes. After a while, Corrie recognized her. She was the nurse who had treated Corrie's dying sister with great cruelty. Corrie admits: 'When I saw her, a feeling of bitterness, almost hatred, came into my heart. How my dying sister had suffered because of her!'

Corrie knew that her duty as a Christian was to forgive this woman. She struggled, but she could not do it. 'Lord, you know I cannot forgive her. My sister suffered too much because of her cruelties.'

At the suggestion of a friend, Corrie invited this nurse to attend the meeting the following night. 'During the entire meeting she looked into my eyes while I spoke. After the meeting, I had a talk with her. I told her that I had been bitter, but that God's Holy Spirit in me had brought His love instead of hatred and that now I loved her . . . I told her more and at the end of our talk that nurse accepted Jesus Christ as her personal Saviour and Lord.'

Just as God, by his Spirit, changed Corrie ten Boom's bitterness into love, so he longs to cultivate within the life of each Christian the fruit of the Spirit which we have examined this week.

If this is to happen we must 'Be filled with the spirit' (Ephesians 5:18).

There is value during the retreat of Lent, in particular, in asking ourselves some searching questions:

> Am I truly loving?
> Am I joyful?
> Am I a peaceful person?
> Have I learned patience?
> Do I exercise kindness, gentleness and goodness?
> Am I self-controlled?

The reason for putting these questions to ourselves is not so that we might become depressed by our dismal failures but rather that the Holy Spirit might reveal to us where we are making progress and which areas he would have us work on next. The Holy Spirit's work is to challenge us, to convict us and to enable us to change. When a person is willing to be changed, the Holy Spirit can effect remarkable transformations.

Father, this week you have shown me myself and where I need to change. Thank you that you do not leave me to bring about these changes on my own but you fill me with your Spirit, the one who co-operates with me to bring about the necessary transformation. I want to change, dear Lord. I want to become more like you. But I know that I cannot do this on my own. So fill me with your Spirit day by day. Keep me from despondency or despair when the going seems tough or when I seem to change, oh, so slowly. Keep before me your plan for my life: to change me from glory into glory; to set me free to become the person you always wanted me to be.

Gracious Spirit, dwell with me!
I myself would gracious be;
And with words that help and heal
Would Thy life in mine reveal;
And with actions bold and meek
Would for Christ, my Saviour, speak.

Thomas Toke Lynch

Jesus' love

Lent is a time for pondering on God's love – a time to try to drink it in.

I once read a story which helps me to understand this love a little better. The story is of a young angel who was being shown round the splendours and glories of the universe by a more experienced angel. The little angel was shown whirling galaxies and blazing suns, infinite distances in interstellar space and, finally, the galaxy of which our own planetary system is a part. As the two of them drew near to the star which we call our sun and to its circling planets, the senior angel pointed to planet Earth. To the little angel whose mind was still full of the grandeur and glory he'd just seen, this planet looked as dull and dirty as a tennis ball.

'What's special about that one?' he asked.

'That,' replied his senior solemnly, 'is the Visited Planet. That ball, which to you looks so insignificant, has been visited by the Prince of Glory.'

'Do you mean to say,' queried the younger one, 'that our great and glorious Prince, with all these wonders and splendours of his creation, and millions more that I'm sure I haven't seen yet, went down in person to this fifth-rate little ball? Why should he do a thing like that?'

'He did it because he loves the people there,' replied the senior angel. 'He went down to visit them so that he could lift them up to become like him.'

The little angel looked blank. Such thoughts were quite beyond his comprehension. Even so it is true:

'God loved the world so much that he gave his only Son... to be the means by which our sins are forgiven.'
John 3:16 and 1 John 4:10

Thank you, Lord, for loving me.

Drinking in God's love

Perfect love is what God is. This love is constant. It never grows tired and never gives up. To be in touch with God is to be in touch with love and held by it.

O the deep, deep love of Jesus!
Vast, unmeasured, boundless, free;
Rolling as a mighty ocean
In its fullness over me.
Underneath me, all around me,
Is the current of Thy love;
Leading onward, leading homeward,
To Thy glorious rest above.
Samuel Trevor Francis

'How precious it is, Lord, to realize that you are thinking about me constantly! I can't even count how many times a day your thoughts turn towards me. And when I wake in the morning, you are still thinking of me!'
Psalm 139:17,18

Suffering love

It wasn't easy for Jesus to die for me. That realization dawned on me when I was in Israel one Lent. I was sitting by the Sea of Galilee, meditating on some verses from Luke's Gospel:

'Jesus took the twelve disciples aside and said to them, "Listen! We are going to Jerusalem where everything the prophets wrote about the Son of Man will come true. He will be handed over to the Gentiles, who will mock him, insult him, and spit on him. They will whip him and kill him..." '

Luke 18:31-33

I wonder how Jesus felt when the time came for him to tear himself away from this place to go up to Jerusalem knowing what would happen to him. I turned that question over and over in my mind as I watched the sun play on the calm lake.

It was Palm Sunday and my husband and I were spinning out our last two hours in the sun before tearing ourselves away from Galilee and travelling up to Jerusalem. I dreaded the thought of exchanging the warmth and stillness of the lakeside for the chill and bustle of the city. How much more heavy hearted Jesus must have been when he turned his back on Galilee and set his face towards Calvary.

As we journeyed to Jerusalem by bus later that day, I thought of the way Jesus had warned his disciples of his impending death. He knew that Jews and Gentiles alike would spit in his face, laugh him to scorn as though he were a buffoon, and hit him so hard with their clenched fists that their blows would cause him to double up with pain. He also knew that his scourged and flogged body would be strung up on the cross. Yet he went through with it. Why? It was love. Pure love:

'The Son of God... loved me and gave himself for me.'

Galatians 2:20

Thank you, Lord, that though it cost you so much,
you did die for me.

Rescuing love

When God first created mankind, he intended that an intimate relationship should exist between the Creator and his creatures. But the first man and woman chose to disobey God and therefore forfeited the privilege of this close friendship. Moreover, through their disobedience, sin made its entry into the world. This sin gave Satan the firm foothold he had been looking for. Sin and Satan now held the world in a vice-like grip. God's people now walked in darkness: oppressed by Satan. Spiritually speaking, they lived in a never-ending winter: rarely experiencing the warmth of God's love. Enslaved by sin as they were, they were doomed to die both physically and spiritually.

> '(Adam's) sin brought death with it. As a result, death has spread to the whole human race because everyone has sinned.'
> Romans 5:12

Jesus knew the solution to the sin-problem. He, the man-who-never-sinned, would need to take upon himself every sin each individual in the world had ever committed and would ever commit. It would be as though he himself had committed the crimes of the cosmos. He would therefore pay the penalty of sin in person. He would die.

> We may not know, we cannot tell,
> What pains He had to bear;
> But we believe it was for us
> He hung and suffered there.
>
> There was no other good enough
> To pay the price of sin;
> He only could unlock the gate
> Of heaven, and let us in.
> Cecil Frances Alexander

Crucified love

When I survey the wondrous cross,
On which the Prince of glory died,
My richest gain I count but loss,
And pour contempt on all my pride.
Isaac Watts

The composer of that well-loved hymn challenges us, not simply to cast a cursory glance at the cross, but to gaze at it reverently and with adoration. We can do that today by looking long and hard and lovingly at this picture of the crucifixion. The nails remind us that men split Jesus' hands and feet as they pinned him to the death gibbet. The ropes remind us that he was hoisted on high for all to see – despised and mocked by those he had come to rescue.

'Without beauty, without majesty (we saw him),
no looks to attract our eyes;
a thing despised and rejected by men,
a man of sorrows and familiar with suffering,
a man to make people screen their faces...
We thought of him as someone punished,
struck by God, and brought low.
Yet he was pierced through for our faults,
crushed for our sins.
On him lies a punishment that brings us peace,
and through his wounds we are healed.'
Isaiah 53:2-5

Lord Jesus, help me to drink in these facts:

Mine were the sufferings you bore
Mine the sorrows you carried
You were pierced through for my faults
Crushed because of my sin
God laid on you the punishment that brought me
Peace, joy and a whole new start in life
Help me to live an adequate
Thank you.

Forgiving love

Look back at the picture of the crucifixion we were contemplating yesterday. Recall how Jesus' body had been scourged and flogged before the crude cross had been loaded onto his torn and bleeding back. Remember how he had stumbled through the cobbled streets of Jerusalem to the hill of Calvary. Look again at those ten-inch nails which had been driven through his hands and his feet. Imagine how it might feel to touch that cruel crown of thorns which pierced his brow. Then listen to that cry of love which silences the swearing of the soldiers:

'Father, forgive them; they do not know what they are doing.'
Luke 23:33

What a prayer to pray over your persecutors! Jesus prayed it because, even in this hour of physical torture, what he most wanted was that his tormentors and you and I should enjoy the peace with God he was purchasing for us on the cross.

> See from his head, his hands, his feet,
> Sorrow and love flow mingled down;
> Did e'er such love and sorrow meet,
> Or thorns compose so rich a crown?
> Isaac Watts

Love and sorrow had never before merged in this way. Neither had thorns from the hedgerow formed such a magnificent crown. But then, never before had God hung on a tree.

> *Lord Jesus, poor and abject, unknown and despised,*
> *Love bound you to that tree, love for mankind,*
> *Love for me.*
> *Lord Jesus, hanging on the accursed tree,*
> *Bowing your head, forgiving me*
> *Let me not be ashamed to follow thee*
> *Now and into eternity.*
> After John Wesley

Beckoning love

The love of Jesus which beckons us from the cross demands a response:

> 'Every advantage that I had gained I considered lost for
> Christ's sake. Yes, and I look upon everything as loss
> compared with the overwhelming gain of knowing Christ
> Jesus my Lord.'
>
> Philippians 3:7-9

A man called Ron once told me why he boasts about Christ's cross. Ron was a paratrooper in the Second World War. On New Year's Eve, 1944, his battalion stayed in an Abbey in France and one of the monks gave him a metal crucifix. On the morning of 24 March 1945, Ron pushed this crucifix in his battledress pocket as he rushed for reveille. That day his battalion crossed the Rhine by plane and were then commanded to jump. Even as he landed, Ron's parachute was punctured by a burst of bullets and his body was spun round by the force of the fire. But he was able to run, unhurt, and shelter in a trench. He found bullet holes in his smock, his battledress and his shirt – but it was two days later, as he stripped for a bath in a military hospital, that he discovered why he had escaped injury.

Embedded in his clothes he found the spent bullet which had cut holes in his clothes. He also drew out of his pocket the metal crucifix which was now broken in two and he realized that this cross had taken the full impact of the bullet and had protected his body from being punctured like his parachute. That was over forty years ago but Ron still thanks God every day for a life which might have ended in 1945.

The hymnwriter recognized that, in a spiritual sense, we, too, have been saved by Christ's cross. That's why he finished his famous hymn with these words:

> Forbid it, Lord, that I should boast
> Save in the cross of Christ my God;
> All the vain things that charm me most,
> I sacrifice them to His blood...
>
> Were the whole realm of nature mine
> That were an offering far too small;
> Love so amazing, so divine,
> Demands my soul, my life, my all.
>
> Isaac Watts

Ransomed

This week, we focus on what Christ's death on the cross achieved. A true story of self-sacrificing love helps me to catch a glimpse of its effectiveness.

A man was once caught stealing from his employers. When the court case was heard, the judge imposed a fine of £50. Failure to pay the prescribed fine, he said, would result in imprisonment.

The night of the court hearing, the man despaired. He had no money. That was why he had resorted to stealing in the first place. How was he to pay the fine? The thought of a period in prison filled him with horror.

Next morning, a brown envelope fell through this man's letter-box. It contained ten, crisp, new five-pound notes and a hand-written explanation: To pay off the debt.

The offender never discovered where the money had come from. The only information he could glean was that a member of the nearby church heard of his plight and decided to set him free from the threat of imprisonment.

When Jesus died on the cruel cross, he bought our release from the clutches of the Evil One. He also set us free from the bondage to sin in which we had been trapped. And he delivered us from the effects of the sin-stained past and from the guilt that enshrouded us:

> The death of Christ: 'One act of perfect righteousness, presents all men freely acquitted in the sight of God.'
> Romans 5:18

> 'God loved the world so much that he gave his only Son, that everyone who has faith in him may not die but have eternal life.'
> John 3:16

We are required only to accept his gift.

He left his Father's throne above,
So free, so infinite His grace;
Emptied Himself of all but love,
And bled for Adam's helpless race;
'Tis mercy all, immense and free;
For, O my God, it found out me.

Long my imprisoned spirit lay
Fast bound in sin and nature's night;
Thine eyes diffused a quickening ray,
I woke, the dungeon flamed with light;
My chains fell off, my heart was free;
I rose, went forth and followed Thee.

No condemnation now I dread;
Jesus, and all in Him, is mine!
Alive in Him, my living Head,
And clothed in righteousness Divine,
Bold I approach th'eternal throne,
And claim the crown, through Christ my own.

Charles Wesley

*From the deep places of my soul, I praise you, O
God:*
I lift up my heart and glorify your holy name.
*From the deep places of my soul, I praise you, O
God:*
how can I forget all your goodness towards me?
You forgive all my sin, you heal all my weaknesses,
you rescue me from the brink of disaster,
you crown me with mercy and compassion . . .
For you have triumphed over the power of death,
and draw us to your presence with songs of joy . . .
From the widest bounds of the universe
to the depths of my very being,
the whispers and cries of joy
vibrate to a shining glory
O God, our beginning and our end.

Jim Cotter

Healed

We all need to know that we are loved. The words: 'I love you' are among the most healing we can ever say to anyone if we really mean what we are saying.

Jesus' sacrificial death on the cross brings emotional healing to many hurting people because it conveys more effectively than any words, the fact that he loves us:

> 'In human experience it is a rare thing for one man to give his life for another, even if the latter be a good man, though there have been a few who have had the courage to do it. Yet the proof of God's amazing love is this: that it was while we were sinners that Christ died for us.'
>
> Romans 5:7-8

Christians know that God loves them because the historical fact of Jesus' death provides them with objective proof of this amazing good news.

But God does not leave it at that. He provides us with subjective evidence that his love for us is intimate:

> 'Already we have some experience of the love of God flooding through our hearts by the Holy Spirit given to us.'
>
> Romans 5:5

In other words, God's healing love is to be felt as well as to be believed intellectually:

'Look at the cross and accept it as God's own proof that He loves you. Ask him to go on flooding your heart with His love through the indwelling Spirit. And then away with gloomy fears! Let them be swallowed up in the steadfast love of God.'
John Stott

'Thanks be to you, our Lord Jesus Christ,
for all the benefits which you have given us,
for all the pains and insults which you have borne
    for us.
Most merciful Redeemer, Friend and Brother,
may we know you more clearly,
love you more dearly,
and follow you more nearly,
day by day.'

Prayer of St Richard

Restored

When the mother of two toddlers was admitted to hospital prior to the birth of her third child, her doctor examined her and predicted a normal delivery and a big, bouncing baby. That night, the woman gave birth, but the labour was both prolonged and painful. Consequently, she was sedated heavily.

Next morning, the mother was shocked to learn that the baby she had given birth to was dead: stillborn, she was told. The hospital staff sympathized with her in her bereavement but advised her to return home and enjoy her other two children. Grief-stricken, the young woman left hospital, and for nine months mourned the loss of the child she had wanted so much.

In the ninth month, detectives knocked at the door of the woman's home and asked her to accompany them to a certain house bringing her other children with her. At the house, the woman saw a little girl, about nine months old, playing happily. Intuitively, this young woman knew that the child was *her* baby. She opened her arms, caught up the child and cuddled her lovingly.

The detectives smiled, observed the striking likeness between the baby and the woman's other children and then explained the mystery. The child in her arms was, indeed, her child. While she had been under sedation after her delivery, a psychiatric patient had crept into the ward and had exchanged her stillborn baby for this woman's healthy child. For the past nine months this woman had brought up the child as though she were her own.

Through a mysterious sequence of events, the deceit had at last been uncovered. So the delighted, rightful mother was allowed to take her baby home knowing that, now her baby had been restored to her, their relationship could begin.

What happened when Jesus gave his life for us at Calvary was that we were restored to a right relationship with God. Intimacy with him became a possibility once more. We were even accepted into God's family circle:

'Let us grasp the fact that we have peace with God through
our Lord Jesus Christ. Through him we have confidently
entered into this new relationship of grace, and here we take
our stand, in happy certainty of the glorious things he has for
us in the future.'

Romans 5:1

'You have been adopted into the very family circle of God and you can say with a full heart, "Father, my Father". The Spirit himself endorses our inward conviction that we really are the children of God. Think what that means. If we are his children we share his treasures, and all that Christ claims as his will belong to all of us as well!'

Romans 8:14

Abba Father, let me be
Yours and yours alone.
Let my will for ever be
Evermore your own.
Never let my heart grow cold,
Never let me go.
Abba Father, let me be
Yours and yours alone.

Forgiven

True forgiveness involves letting the offending person off the hook. It includes bearing injury without retaliation. It means continuing to accept the person who has inflicted the hurt or pain. And it involves continuing to love without reserve.

Because of Jesus' death at Calvary, we can know the joy of being on the receiving end of such forgiveness:

'God has now made you to share in the very life of Christ! He has forgiven you all your sins: Christ has utterly wiped out the damning evidence of broken laws and commandments which always hung over our heads, and has completely annulled it by nailing it over his own head on the cross. And then, having drawn the sting of all the powers ranged against us, he exposed them, shattered, empty and defeated, in his final glorious triumphant act!'

Colossians 2:13-15

Praise, my soul, the King of heaven,
To His feet thy tribute bring;
Ransomed, healed, restored, forgiven,
Who like thee his praise should sing?
Praise Him! Praise Him!
Praise the everlasting King!

Henry Francis Lyte

Cleansed

The blood of Jesus is the best detergent in the world. When we apply it to our sins and mistakes and failures, it erases the stain completely and leaves us free to live before God and before others as though we had never ever sinned.

'Come now, let us talk this over,
says Yahweh.
Though your sins are like scarlet,
they shall be as white as snow;
though they are red as crimson,
they shall be like wool.'
Isaiah 1:18

'We face God as we are: sinful, spiritually handicapped and disabled in many ways, chronic patients. And we accept these handicaps and disabilities because he accepts us as we are, and because he loves us as we are.

'We are not permitted to nurse a sense of guilt; we must fully and completely accept and embrace his forgiveness and love. Guilt feeling and inferiority before God are expressions of selfishness, of self-centredness: we give greater importance to our little sinful self than to his immense and never-ending love. We must surrender our guilt and inferiority to him; his goodness is greater than our badness. We must surrender our sinfulness to his mercy.'
James Borst

'Happy are those whose wrongs are forgiven,
whose sins are pardoned!
Happy is the person whose sins the Lord
will not keep account of!'
Psalm 32:1,2

Lord, what joy you give me. I come to you penitent,
able only to cry over my sin, and ask you for help.
You come to me offering unlimited forgiveness,
sufficient grace to cancel all my sin. For a love
which sees the full horror of my failure and yet
which goes on caring and forgiving, I thank you
and rejoice from the depths of my being.

Released

The death of Jesus has cancelled out the effect of our sin-stained past. But it does more than this. It even deals with the guilt. Paul puts it this way:

> 'God did not keep back his own Son, but offered him for us all!... Who will accuse God's chosen people? God himself declares them not guilty! Can anyone then condemn them?'
>
> Romans 8:32-33

'Not guilty!' That's the good news. Because a guilty person lives with the dread that their past misdemeanours will yet be discovered. The guilty person is at enmity with himself, with others and with God. The guilty person often becomes an anxious person. But all that can change since the death of Jesus is capable of dealing with our guilt.

An elderly lady I once met testified to this fact as she told me her story. She lived 'a terrible life' but, aware that she was growing old, she decided that she would like to live near her grandchildren. 'But,' she reasoned, 'my daughter knows the kind of life I've led. Maybe she wouldn't want her mother so near? After all, I could influence her children, couldn't I?' One day she told her daughter what was on her mind and her daughter's response took her by surprise: 'Why don't you put your trust in Jesus, Mummy? He can wipe out the past, set you free from it, and give you a completely new start.'

'At first, I hardly dared believe what she told me,' the old lady said. 'But I thought it was worth a try. So I told God I was sorry for the past. I asked him to forgive me. And d'you know what happened? He forgave me. He set me free from all that filth and evil. *Even the guilt has gone.* I didn't realize it was possible to be so happy. He's given me such joy. And I don't deserve it after what I've done.'

'Even the guilt has gone!' Thank you, Lord, that though I, too, have failed you so many times, when you look at me, you see, not my sin and guilt but the dying form of your Son, so in your sight I am 'not guilty'. Teach me to be a responsible steward of such dearly-bought freedom.

Saved

We end this week as we began – with a true story which illustrates what Christ's death on the cross achieved. The story is of Natalie, a Russian woman of whom little is known except her name and the fact that she lived in Russia when civil war ravaged that country.

As war swept through the land, the wife of an officer in the White Army knew that she and her children must hide because the city where she lived had fallen into the hands of the Red Army. She hid in a small, wooden cabin on the outskirts of the city.

Towards evening on her second day in hiding, she heard a knock on the cabin door. On the doorstep stood a young woman of her own age. The woman spoke in whispers but urged the mother to leave that night with her children. 'You've been discovered,' she said. 'Tonight they will come.'

The mother looked down at her two small children. How could she escape? They would quickly be caught.

'Don't worry about the children. I'll stay here. They won't even look for you.'

That night, the woman, Natalie, came back. The mother and her two small boys escaped into the woods. Natalie faced the certainty of death alone. With the cold of morning the soldiers came. They battered down the door and, without checking her identity, shot her just where she was. Next day, she was found by friends – dead.

Natalie could have escaped from that cabin at any time. She chose not to. She died so that others might live.

Almost two thousand years before, a man of Natalie's age – Jesus – rode into Jerusalem to do something similar for us. He took upon himself all the guilt and horror of our sin. He suffered the whole weight of the judgement that was due to us. He sacrificed his own life so that ours might be saved.

> 'We all, like sheep, have gone astray,
> each of us has turned to his own way;
> and the Lord has laid on him
> the iniquity of us all.'
> Isaiah 53:6

Ride on! ride on in majesty!
In lowly pomp ride on to die;
O Christ, Thy triumphs now begin
O'er captive death and conquered sin.

Ride on! ride on in majesty!
The angel armies of the sky
Look down with sad and wondering eyes
To see the approaching sacrifice.

Ride on! ride on in majesty!
The last and fiercest strife is nigh;
The Father on His sapphire throne
Awaits His own anointed Son.

Ride on! ride on in majesty!
In lowly pomp ride on to die;
Bow Thy meek head to mortal pain,
Then take, O God, Thy power, and reign.

Henry Hart Milman

Christ triumphant

This week, Holy Week, we examine some of the events of the last week of Jesus' life and seek to understand what it cost him to go to the gallows.

'As he was approaching Bethphage and Bethany, near the hill called the Mount of Olives, he sent off two of his disciples telling them, "Go into the village just ahead of you, and there you will find a colt tied, on which no one has ever yet ridden. Untie it and bring it here. And if anybody asks you, "Why are you untying it?" just say, "The Lord needs it." So the messengers went off and found things just as he had told them. In fact, as they were untying the colt, the owners did say, "Why are you untying it?" and they replied, "The Lord needs it." So they brought it to Jesus and, throwing their cloaks upon it, mounted Jesus on its back. Then as he rode along, people spread out their coats in the roadway. And as he approached the city, where the road sloped down from the Mount of Olives, the whole crowd of disciples joyfully shouted praises to God for all the marvellous things they had seen him do. "God bless the king who comes in the name of the Lord!" they cried. "There is peace in Heaven and glory on high!" '

Luke 19:29-38

Jesus knew when he entered Jerusalem with such a flourish that he was taking a double risk: the risk of death and the risk of rejection. He knew that there was a price on his head; that the religious leaders had laid traps for him. He knew, too, that in asking the question: 'Will you take me as your King?' he was inviting the reaction of the majority which would be an unequivocal 'No'.

Lord Jesus, at the beginning of this Holy Week, I want to reaffirm your lordship over my life. Take the reins and lead me where you will. Take everything I have and everything I am and do with me what you will. May my life glorify your name, now and always.

Jesus cleanses the Temple

If the manner of Jesus' entry into Jerusalem was both courageous and defiant in the light of the fact that he was a marked man, his cleansing of the Temple on the Monday of Holy Week was even more daring. Mark tells the story vividly:

'They came into Jerusalem and Jesus went into the Temple and began to drive out those who were buying and selling there. He overturned the tables of the money-changers and the benches of the dove-sellers, and he would not allow people to carry their water-pots through the Temple. And he taught them and said, "Doesn't the scripture say, 'My house shall be called a house of prayer for all the nations'? But you have turned it into a thieves' kitchen!" '

Mark 11:15-17

The Temple had been built as a house of prayer for all nations. But Gentiles were only allowed in one outer court which the Jews abused by using it as a thoroughfare and for trade. It was always thronging with people and it had become the scene of double-dealings which outraged Jesus. The money-changers whose booths dominated these outer precincts of the Temple fleeced pilgrims by placing a heavy surcharge on every transaction they made. And the dove-sellers were equally deceitful. They charged extortionate prices for their wares but rejected any doves bought elsewhere on the grounds that these were blemished and were therefore unfit offerings for God. With a ruthlessness that must have astonished all his onlookers, Jesus rid the Temple of these practices which could never co-exist with a holy God.

Lord, your word reminds me that I, too, am a temple; that your Spirit has taken up residence inside me. This Holy Week, deal ruthlessly with me. Show me what needs dealing with in my life – which behaviour patterns, attitudes and failures of mine cannot co-exist with your Spirit. Then give me the courage to deal ruthlessly with them – before Easter Day dawns.

The betrayal

During Holy Week, Jesus suffered the pain of rejection, not simply from the religious leaders of the day, nor simply from the crowds who thronged the streets of Jerusalem. Even his own disciples failed to understand his mission and, by their actions, added to his pain. Luke places the spotlight on Judas and shows how he colluded with the enemies of Jesus:

'Now as the feast of unleavened bread, called the Passover, was approaching, fear of the people made the chief priests and scribes try desperately to find a way of getting rid of Jesus. Then a diabolical plan came into the mind of Judas Iscariot, who was one of the twelve. He went and discussed with the chief priests and officers a method of getting Jesus into their hands. They were delighted and arranged to pay him for it. He agreed, and began to look for a suitable opportunity for betrayal when there was no crowd present.'

Luke 22:1-5

It was the ambition of every Jew in the world to be present in Jerusalem at Passover time at least once in his lifetime. Because of this, vast numbers of people flocked to the holy city for the festival. The atmosphere was always inflammable. The Jewish authorities knew this and determined to arrest Jesus before the feast to avoid a riot. And Judas played right into their hands, offering to lead them to Jesus at an appropriate time and an appropriate place.

But Judas was not the only disciple to fail his master during the last hours of Jesus' earthly ministry. Jesus knew that, when he needed his support most, even Peter would turn deserter. He warned Peter of this:

'Simon Peter said to him, "Lord, where are you going?"
"I am going,' replied Jesus, ' where you cannot follow me now, though you will follow me later."
"Lord, why can't I follow you now?" said Peter. "I would lay down my life for you!"
"Would you lay down your life for me?" replied Jesus.
"Believe me, you will disown me three times before the cock crows."'

John 13:36-38

And before the first Good Friday had dawned, each of Jesus' disciples
had abandoned him to his fate. Matthew records the sad fact that
after Jesus' arrest:

> 'All the disciples left him and ran away.'
> Matthew 26:56

In the Book of Lamentations, we read a poem which is thought by
some to predict the sufferings Jesus endured during this last week of
his life:

> 'Is it nothing to you, all you who pass by?
> Look around and see.
> Is any suffering like my suffering
> that was inflicted on me? . . .
> This is why I weep
> and my eyes overflow with tears.
> No one is near to comfort me,
> no one to restore my spirit
> People have heard my groaning,
> but there is no one to comfort me.
> All my enemies have heard my distress;
> they rejoice at what you have done.'
> Lamentations 1:12,16,21

Lord, when chosen friends reject or disown me, or
when they fail to give me the comfort I crave, I sting
all over. This obscenity of Judas – exchanging you
for thirty silver coins – and this cowardice which
caused your other friends to flee must have caused
you similar pain. You knew it would happen yet you
loved them enough patiently to endure this pain. I
cannot understand such love and courage. Help me
to understand it.

> O make me understand it,
> Help me to take it in,
> What it meant to Thee, the Holy One,
> To bear away my sin.
> Katherine A.M. Kelly

The last supper

Just as, at Christmas time, Christians celebrate the birth of Jesus, so at Passover time, the Jews celebrate the occasion when God delivered their nation from Egypt where they had been enslaved. The Passover Feast was one of the highlights of the year and Jesus longed to share this special meal with his closest friends, his disciples.

The disciples were never to forget this particular occasion, partly because it was to prove to be the last meal they would eat with Jesus before his death and partly because of the things Jesus did on this occasion. John describes one of the surprises Jesus sprung on that particular evening:

> 'Jesus . . . rose from the supper-table, took off his outer clothes, picked up a towel and fastened it around his waist. Then he poured water into the basin and began to wash the disciples' feet and to dry them with the towel around his waist . . . When Jesus had washed their feet and put on his clothes, he sat down again and spoke to them: "Do you realize what I have just done to you? You call me 'teacher' and 'Lord' and are quite right, for I am your teacher and your Lord. But if I, your teacher and Lord, have washed your feet, you must be ready to wash one another's feet. I have given you this example so that you may do as I have done.'
> John 13:4-15

In washing his friends' feet, Jesus had performed the most menial task imaginable. His challenge to us is: 'Love one another as I have loved you.'

Like every host at this particular meal, Jesus took bread and distributed it to his friends. Then he took a cup of wine and blessed it. But Luke reminds us that the words Jesus used on this occasion were unique.

> 'Then he took a loaf and after thanking God he broke it and gave it to them with these words, "This is my body which is given for you: do this in remembrance of me." So too, he gave them a cup after supper with the words, "This cup is the new agreement made in my own blood which is shed for you."'
> Luke 22:19

Jesus knew what the disciples did not yet know, that on the very next day, his body would literally be broken and his blood spilled. He was about to sacrifice his life as a once-and-for-all offering for sin. It was to be a kind of charter sealed with his own blood which would dwarf any other previous attempts to bring God and man together. *This* agreement, steeped as it was in sacrifice, would reconcile God and man for ever. *This* agreement would secure man's forgiveness from sin. *This* agreement proved that God's love for mankind was unquenchable.

> *Remove from me, dear Lord, the heart of stone that*
> *can contemplate these mysteries without awe,*
> *without wonder, and without a response of adoring*
> *love. Give me, instead, a heart that warms with*
> *gratitude whenever I reflect on the fact that you, the*
> *Son of God, signed the agreement which reconciled*
> *me to a pure and holy God with your own life-blood,*
> *freely shed out of love for me.*

> Man of Sorrows! what a name
> For the Son of God, who came
> Ruined sinners to reclaim!
> Hallelujah! What a Saviour!
> Philipp Bliss

The Garden of Gethsemane

On several occasions I have knelt in the Garden of Gethsemane and tried to imagine how Jesus might have felt on the night before he died. But no one can hope to identify fully with the anguish the Son of God must have suffered as he pleaded with his Father to show him an escape route from the cross of Calvary. The Gospel writers give us a glimpse of some of the pain and turmoil which caused Jesus to plead with the Father to deliver him from the necessity of dying the death of a criminal. Matthew records some of Jesus' feelings:

'Then Jesus went with his disciples to a place called Gethsemane, and he said to them, "Sit here while I go over there and pray." He took with him Peter and the two sons of Zebedee. Grief and anguish came over him, and he said to them, "The sorrow in my heart is so great that it almost crushes me. Stay here and keep watch with me."'
Matthew 26:36-38

Matthew goes on to reveal the struggle Jesus had to accept the task which lay before him: that of bearing the loathsome burden of our sin in his own body on the cross:

'He went a little further on, threw himself face downwards on the ground, and prayed, "My Father, if it is possible, take this cup of suffering from me! Yet not what I want, but what you want."
Then he returned to the three disciples and found them asleep; and he said to Peter, "How is it that you three were not able to keep watch with me even for one hour? Keep watch and pray . . ."
Once more Jesus went away and prayed, "My Father, if this cup of suffering cannot be taken away unless I drink it, your will be done." He returned once more and found the disciples asleep; they could not keep their eyes open.'
Matthew 26:39-43

Luke describes even more graphically the agony Jesus encountered while he prayed:

'In great anguish he prayed . . . his sweat was like drops of blood falling to the ground.'
Luke 22:44

The Son of God gripped by fear!
The Son of God crushed by a killing sorrow!
The Son of God in anguish!
The Son of God sweating great drops of blood!
The Son of God shuddering in the face of death!
The Son of God shrinking at the cost of the Cross!
It was not easy for Jesus to die for me.

'He did not want to die. He was thirty-three and no one wants to die
with life just opening onto the best of the years . . . He had to compel
himself to go on.
William Barclay

'O Jesus, by thy bonds of love
draw me to your Cross and bind me there,
lest I waste all and cause you further pain.'
Gilbert Shaw

> It is a thing most wonderful,
> Almost too wonderful to be,
> That God's own Son should come from heaven,
> And die to save a child like me.
>
> And yet I know that it is true;
> He chose a poor and humble lot,
> And wept, and toiled, and mourned, and died
> For love of those who loved Him not.
>
> I sometimes think about the cross,
> And shut my eyes, and try to see
> The cruel nails, and crown of thorns,
> And Jesus crucified for me.
>
> But even could I see Him die,
> I could but see a little part
> Of that great love, which, like a fire,
> Is always burning in His heart.
>
> It is most wonderful to know
> His love for me so free and sure;
> But 'tis more wonderful to see
> My love for Him so faint and poor.
>
> And yet I want to love Thee, Lord;
> O light the flame within my heart,
> And I will love Thee more and more,
> Until I see Thee as Thou art.
> William Walsham How

Jesus is crucified

Judas went through with his plan. He knew Jesus well enough to suspect that it would be to the Garden of Gethsemane that he would retreat. It was there that he betrayed his Master with a traitor's kiss. Throughout Thursday night, Jesus stood trial. Although Pilate, the Roman governor, could find no cause for imposing the death penalty, he capitulated to the crowd's clamour when he presented Jesus to them:

'Crucify him!'

'Then the governor's soldiers took Jesus into the governor's palace and collected the whole guard around him. They twisted some thorn-twigs into a crown and put it on his head and put a stick into his right hand. They bowed low before him and jeered at him with the words: "Hail, your majesty, king of the Jews!" Then they spat on him, took the stick and hit him on the head with it. And when they had finished their fun, they stripped the cloak off again, put his own clothes upon him and led him off for crucifixion. On their way out of the city they met a man called Simon, a native of Cyrene in Africa, and they compelled him to carry Jesus' cross.'

Matthew 27:27-32

'A huge crowd of people followed him, including women who wrung their hands and wept for him . . . Two criminals were also led out with him for execution, and when they came to the place called The Skull, they crucified him with the criminals, one on either side of him . . .
It was now about midday, but darkness came over the whole countryside until three in the afternoon, for there was an eclipse of the sun. The veil in the Temple sanctuary was split in two. Then Jesus gave a great cry and said,
"Father, I commend my spirit into your hands."
And with these words he died.'

Luke 23:27-46

'They hammered nails into the wood through his hands, they split his feet through cutting into the rough cross.
Helpless he was hoisted, a shame and a mockery of a man, pinned to a death gibbet . . .
They had won. Destroyed, rejected, broken,
his very person seemed to have been shattered,
no one would follow his teaching,

88

or believe anything he had said any more.
His mother, Mary, with Mary Magdalene and John, stood by,
and millions of others of all times and nations,
who believed in Him as the Beloved Son of God.'
Desmond Sullivan

Today he who hung the earth upon the waters is hung upon the Cross.
He who is King of the angels is arrayed in a crown of thorns.
He who wraps the heaven in clouds is wrapped in the purple of mockery.
He who in Jordan set Adam free receives blows upon his face.
The Bridegroom of the Church is transfixed with nails.
The Son of the Virgin is pierced with a spear.
We worship you, Lord Jesus.
Draw us to yourself with bands of love.
Show us the glory of your Resurrection.
Adaptation of Hymns of Good Friday, Orthodox Tradition

The disciples wait

On Easter Saturday, or Holy Saturday, I like to try to identify with the feelings the first disciples must have had on that day which followed so closely on the traumatic events of Good Friday. They had discovered that Joseph of Arimathea had gained permission from Pilate to remove the body of Jesus from the cross and to embalm and bury it. The women had followed Joseph, taking careful note of the particular tomb in which he had placed Jesus. But then, because it was the Jewish Sabbath when they were not permitted to work or to travel, they were forced to spend their day waiting impatiently for the first possible moment when they could visit the tomb for themselves and give vent to their grief.

What did they do on that Saturday? Did they sit huddled behind locked doors for fear of recrimination from Jesus' enemies? Did they weep and mourn as they re-lived the last agonizing moments of Jesus' life? Did they give voice to the pain which separation from their master must have inflicted on them? Were they restless or frustrated because they could not visit the scene of Jesus' burial earlier? Did they suffer that intolerable emptiness the bereaved person experiences when they have lost a loved one? We are not told. What we do know is that they spent part of the day in preparation. Luke hints at this when he shows that all their preparations were completed before the crack of dawn:

> 'At the first signs of dawn on the first day of the week, they
> went to the tomb taking with them aromatic spices they
> had prepared.'
> Luke 24:1

I also like to mull over the events of Good Friday on this day; to linger, as it were at the foot of the cross, to take time to focus on the astounding fact that the King of Kings and Lord of Lords lies in the grave. I like to try to absorb the meaning of the sacrifice Jesus made, to attempt to express my gratitude that he hung on that tree in my place. Like the composer of this song, I like to take time to meditate on the cross on which Jesus died:

Behold, behold, the wood of the cross
On which is hung our salvation
O come let us adore.
Dan Schutte

Quietness, prayer and confession make us ready to receive the risen
Christ afresh in our hearts.

Give us true repentance;
forgive us our sins of negligence and ignorance
and our deliberate sins;
and grant us the grace of your Holy Spirit
to amend our lives according to your holy word.
Holy God,
holy and strong,
holy and immortal,
have mercy upoh us.
The Alternative Service Book

We are now ready to enter into resurrection joy:

This is the night when Jesus Christ
broke the chains of death
and rose triumphant from the grave.

What good would life have been to us,
had Christ not come as our Redeemer?

Father, how wonderful your care for us!
How boundless your merciful love!

To ransom a slave
you gave away your Son.

O happy fault, O necessary sin of Adam,
which gained for us so great a Redeemer!

Most blessed of all nights, chosen by God
to see Christ rising from the dead! . . .

The power of this holy night
dispels all evil, washes guilt away,
restores lost innocence, brings mourners joy;
it casts out hatred, brings us peace, and humbles earthly pride.

Night truly blessed when Heaven is wedded to earth
and man is reconciled with God!

Therefore, heavenly Father, in the joy of this night,
receive our . . . sacrifices of praise.
The Roman Missal

Christ is risen! Hallelujah!

This good news reverberates around the world today just as joyfully as it was spread from disciple to disciple on that first Easter morning. Matthew captures some of the excitement and awe which characterized this day of days:

'When the Sabbath was over, just as the first day of the week was dawning, Mary from Magdala and the other Mary went to look at the tomb. At that moment there was a great earthquake, for an angel of the Lord came down from Heaven, went forward and rolled back the stone, and took his seat upon it. His appearance was dazzling like lightning and his clothes were white as snow. The guards shook with terror at the sight of him and collapsed like dead men. But the angel spoke to the women, "Do not be afraid. I know that you are looking for Jesus who was crucified. He is not here – he is risen, just as he said he would. Come and look at the place where he was lying. Then go quickly and tell his disciples that he has risen from the dead . . . Then the women went away quickly from the tomb, their hearts filled with awe and great joy, and ran to give the news to his disciples. But quite suddenly, Jesus stood before them in their path, and said, "Peace be with you!" And they went forward to meet him and, clasping his feet, worshipped him.'

Matthew 28:1-19

The women came to the tomb expecting to find a cold corpse. Instead they were found by the living Jesus. Their hearts were filled with sorrowful memories of him dying in weakness. And Christ delights to surprise them with his resurrection strength and joy. They believed that Jesus had been defeated by Satan and by death. Instead, he showed them that he had conquered both. The husk of his humanity could contain the divine Son of God no longer. In the grave, God touched him. He burst through the limitations of his manhood and revealed himself for who he was: the King of Kings and Lord of Lords; the victorious one; the Saviour of the world. And so with confidence we testify:

I know that my Redeemer is alive,
And at the last he will rise upon the earth.
When I awake, he will set me by his side,
And in my flesh, I shall see God.

Job 19:25, quoted from the Liturgy of Taizé

Thine be the glory, risen, conquering Son,
Endless is the victory Thou o'er death hast won;
Angels in bright raiment rolled the stone away,
Kept the folded grave-clothes, where Thy body lay.

Thine be the glory, risen, conquering Son,
Endless is the victory, Thou o'er death hast won.

Lo! Jesus meets us risen from the tomb;
Lovingly he greets us, scatters fear and gloom;
Let the church with gladness, hymns of triumph sing,
For the Lord now liveth, death hath lost its sting.

Thine be the glory, risen, conquering Son,
Endless is the victory, Thou o'er death hast won.

No more we doubt Thee, glorious Prince of life:
Life is nought without Thee; aid us in our strife,
Make us more than conquerors, through Thy deathless love;
Bring us safe through Jordan to Thy home above.

Thine be the glory, risen, conquering Son,
Endless is the victory Thou o'er death hast won.

Edmond Louis Budry translated by Richard Birch Hoyle

Eternal God and Father, by whose power
our Lord Jesus Christ was raised from the dead:
with the whole company of your people in heaven and on earth
we rejoice and give thanks,
that he who was dead is alive again
and lives for evermore;
that he is with us now and always,
and that nothing can part us from your love in him;
that he has opened the way to your kingdom
and brought us the gift of eternal life.
All glory, praise and thanksgiving,
all worship, honour and love,
be yours, almighty and everlasting God,
in time and for all eternity.

New Every Morning

Christ is risen, Alleluia!
The stone has been rolled away, Alleluia!
He is not among the dead anymore, Alleluia!
He has conquered Satan by his death on the Cross, Alleluia!
He has delivered me from the penalty of sin, Alleluia!
My hope and my joy are in him, Alleluia!

Worthy is the Lamb that was slain,
and hath redeemed us to God by his blood,
to receive power, and riches, and wisdom,
and strength, and honour, and glory and blessing. Amen

Revelation 5:12,13, quoted from Handel's *The Messiah*